Inspirations

By

Janice Harvey

To Shirley & George -
May these poems
touch your hearts
and be a blessing
to you.
Janice Harvey

ISBN: 1-4107-1256-7 (e-book)
ISBN: 1-4107-1257-5 (Paperback)

Library of Congress Control Number: 2003090137

This book is printed on acid free paper.

Printed in the United States of America
Bloomington, IN

1stBooks - rev. 06/09/03

DEDICATION

LISA KAYE HARVEY HARRINGTON
April 3, 1967 - December 16, 1996

This book of poems is dedicated to my daughter, Lisa, who was my inspiration for many of the poems here. She was my encourager and supporter. She also loved to write poetry, and this was a very special bond between us.

TABLE OF CONTENTS

YOU PRAYED FOR ME

You brought me there before God's throne,
My trials made your very own,
No longer did I feel alone,
You prayed for me.

Your love for me you chose to share,
Released God's power by your prayer,
And Satan bound within his lair,
You prayed for me.

His strength for me you did avail,
His mercies, they will never fail,
I am assured He will prevail,
You prayed for me.

For me, you sought to intercede,
You were my friend in time of need,
And from my burden I was freed,
You prayed for me.

His love burst through in one bright ray,
It brought assurance in the fray,
And gave me strength to face the day,
You prayed for me.

His presence then I felt so near,
He took away my doubt and fear,
And gave His comfort, oh, so dear,
You prayed for me.

You gave me hope to wait and see,
What God's answer then would be,
To be assured He cares for me,
Because you prayed.

ELEVEN DAYS INTO FORTY YEARS

In Egypt's land, God's children knew
Such persecution cruel,
Unjustly burdened did they strive,
There under Pharaoh's rule.

God had a plan for those He loved,
Relief from Pharaoh's hand.
He, Moses chose to lead them to
A milk and honey land.

Then God on Egypt sent the plagues,
And Pharaoh, filled with fear,
Said, "Moses, take these people now,
And lead them far from here."

A journey of eleven days,
Before them now was laid.
They quickly readied for the trip,
And their provisions made.

God led them in the cloud by day,
And in the fire by night.
In deepest love, He cared for them,
Delivered from each plight.

Upon dry land, He led them through
The depths of the Red Sea.
And Pharaoh's troops were swallowed up,
God's people now were free.

When Moses went upon the mount,
To seek God's will to know,
The people built a golden calf,
And worshipped there below.

Because of sin, God's blessings
To them were oft delayed.
His loving kindness shown to them,
With murm'rings they repaid.

In disobedience they wandered,
Hearts so filled with lust and greed,
Eyes so blind to one who waited,
Ready still to intercede.

Entrenched more deeply in their sin,
Their sorrows multiplied,
And there in that bleak wilderness,
In deep regret they died.

God's yoke is always easy,
His safe pathway the best.
His road is always shortest,
And leads to happiness.

For forty years, they wandered there,
And failed to enter in.
What sad reflection on their lives,
To think what might have been.

BON VOYAGE

Vaya con Dios, is my prayer,
May He in love enfold you.
May He protect, sustain and guide,
And in His strong arms hold you.

And may you know throughout each day,
We're lifting you in prayer,
In love to God's own precious throne,
That He'll your way prepare.

I pray that He may touch your life
With insight fresh and new,
That He may bless beyond your hopes,
Discernment give to you.

May He watch o'er your family here,
As from them you're apart,
And may you know with certainty,
You're held in every heart.

May you come safely back again.
Kept ever in His care.
May wisdom come with knowledge gained,
May you this wisdom share.

Written for Pastor Steve Beigle when leaving for his trip to Russia.

KRISTIN LEE

There's a little girl so precious,
And as yet unseen on earth.
Though by sight, I've yet to know her,
Still she has unmeasured worth.

Now I feel her here within me,
Every movement, oh, so dear.
My heart o'erflows with boundless love,
And I shed a joyful tear.

This child inside, with breath undrawn,
Is a miracle of love,
God created in His wisdom,
Gave a gift from heav'n above.

Anticipation grows so strong,
As I now await her birth,
Praising God for His creation,
As she enters realms of earth.

I long to see her tiny face,
Hold her closely in my arms.
With deepest love will I enfold her,
Guarding her from all life's harms.

I ask for strength to care for her,
Help to teach her in Your will.
With wisdom that is from above,
I now pray my heart you'll fill.

Dear Lord, I pray Your blessing on
All her life that's yet to be,
And ask that You may be my guide,
That she might see You in me!

Written as if by Lisa, as she awaited
Kristie's birth

LISA, MY DAUGHTER

God gave a special gift to me
Some twenty years ago,
A precious little girl child,
And, Oh!, I loved her so!

In her were all my hopes and dreams
I prayed for future bright,
That God would always lead her,
And keep her seeking right.

I've watched her grow from baby-hood,
Still sweeter every day.
Her faith in God so precious,
Has stayed her through the fray.

Life has dealt some tragic blows,
To this sweet child of mine,
But even facing death itself,
Her faith did brightly shine.

Remember what He's done for you,
And never, ever stray.
You're precious to us both, you know.
We love you more each day.

HOMEGOING

God gave her to me for a while,
To love and nurture here,
So oft to bring me great delight,
And sometimes bring a tear.

Please help me Lord, to understand
Why You did call her name,
So young, so dear, so greatly loved
When death's dark angel came.

How hard this final fond farewell,
That lovely voice now still.
How sweet to know we'll meet again,
Where she shall know no ill.

What great rejoicing there will be,
Reunion, oh so sweet,
When once again I hold her close
At our dear Jesus' feet.

She longed for heaven's sweet release,
Earth's pain-filled days are done.
Now in her loving Savior's arms,
My precious child is home!

Lisa Kaye Harvey Harrington
April 3, 1967 - December 16, 1996

I DID NOT DIE

I left the sin-filled world behind,
With troubles that beset mankind,
A better dwelling place to find,
I did not die.

God set me free from earthly pain,
The joys of heaven now to gain,
And untold blessings to attain,
I did not die.

Gone every heartache, every sigh,
As now I dwell with Him on high,
And know His presence ever nigh,
I did not die.

The realms of heaven welcome me,
And loved ones once again I see,
As they extend their arms to me,
I did not die.

I live on still in loving hearts,
As God's sweet comfort He imparts,
And paths of healing freely charts,
I did not die.

And now I see Him face to face,
And fully comprehend His grace,
As into His, my hand I place,
I did not die.

Written as if by Lisa, following her death.

LITTLE MEMORY VERSES FOR LISA

A precious gift from God was she,
Sweet token of His love.
Oh, how it thrills my heart to know,
She *lives* with Him above!

'Twas a melody sweet,
God's loving refrain.
Through the gift of His mercy,
We'll see her again.

She left us for her home on high,
To dwell with God above.
Our sorrow deep in losing her,
O'er shadowed by His love.

As a child she knew the story,
Of Christ's birth by angels told.
Now she sees Him in His glory,
And knows His blessings manifold.

She blessed our lives so briefly here,
Her leaving brought a tear.
We thank God for the years He gave,
And hold her memory dear.

A gift so precious to our hearts,
Was this dear child God gave.
We're thankful, knowing she still lives,
For Jesus came to save.

HAPPY BIRTHDAY, PASTOR

(Now, was that Biegle or Beigle)

Has it been a half century.
Those years two score and ten?
And you're just such a young man,
(This is now - that was then!)

And whence cometh the graying
On the top of the head,
And the glasses on nose perched,
When something is read?

You've so kindly reminded of
Our advancing in years,
That our memory is failing,
And senility rears.

But, 'cause I'm such a nice person,
I would never get even,
So God's blessing I pray on
Dear OLD PASTOR STEPHEN!

NO ROOM IN THE INN

The journey's been long,
The air holds a chill.
Night has descended,
And all is now still.

They've come to the city,
Their journey now ended,
The Inn is in sight,
And rest is expected.

The innkeeper's words
Fall hard on their ears,
And Mary is struggling
To keep back the tears.

"No room in the Inn",
Oh, can it be so?
No room for God's Son,
Now where can they go?

On the door of your heart,
He is knocking today.
Will you give Him room,
Not send Him away?

Will you welcome Him in,
To your heart give the key?
He is God's precious gift
To you and to me.

THE BEST GIFT, JESUS

How crude the manger where He lay,
So helpless and so small,
His majesty forsaken now,
To save man from the fall.

That tiny One who came to us,
With naught of wealth or fame,
And humbly entered realms of earth,
Still bore God's holy name.

He came down from His heav'nly home,
To dwell with human kind,
To suffer man's rejection cruel,
His glory left behind.

The angels served and worshipped Him,
In awe they held His name.
In honor there, He ruled with God,
A kingship He could claim.

Our Lord Emmanuel was He,
Though in a baby's frame,
Delivered there from Mary's womb,
He came to bear our shame.

My finite mind cannot conceive,
Unworthy as I am,
That God, for me, would sacrifice
His precious, holy Lamb.

In thankfulness may we receive
This Greatest Gift e'er given,
In love incomprehensible,
To woo our souls to heaven.

A CHILD IS BORN

He came to me one day as I
Sat quietly alone,
Appearing there so suddenly,
With face that brightly shone.

Who is this one all clothed in white?
My heart responds with fear!
He kindly says, "Don't be afraid,
For God has sent me here.

'In His eyes you've favor found,
And blessed you shall be,
In giving birth to God's own Son,
Salvation bringing free."

The months have passed, and now I feel
His Presence here within.
I thank God that He's giv'n to me
This One who'll save from sin.

A census time has been decreed,
With Joseph I must go,
To Bethlehem to pay the tax,
Which Caesar proclaims due.

With body now so cumbersome,
My steed I climb upon,
And with Joseph, my betrothed,
The journey is begun.

Arriving late in Bethlehem,
So weary to the bone,
I pray to find a place of rest,
And see this long day done.

The innkeeper is kind but firm,
His rooms have been filled all.
He offers us his stable warm
With hay-filled cattle stall.

With barely time to settle in,
I know my hour is near.
In weariness, I lay me down,
So thankful to be here.

And there upon the manger's hay,
Dear Joseph makes a bed,
And quickly readies for this Child,
A place to lay His head.

These months of waiting culminate,
His birth is now at hand,
And as He draws His first deep breath,
I hear the angel band.

Proclaiming joyfully the news,
From far above the earth,
Giving glory to our God,
As they tell of His birth.

As I in wonder hold this Child,
Amazement fills my heart,
That He, all sovereign, would choose me,
To play this vital part!

AS SHEPHERDS WATCHED

They rested on the hillside there,
The day had been so long,
Now, very welcome was the night,
So far from noise-some throng.

The sheep were settled down at last,
The chores of this day o'er,
In weariness they laid them there,
And sleep was near once more.

The earth was calm, the night was still,
When bursting forth in glory,
The sky was rent, the angels came,
And told their ageless story.

A star with brilliance filled the skies,
Their hearts were pricked with fright.
Their strength renewed, they hasted now,
With joy their steps made light.

I sense the thrill, the shepherds' awe,
A stirring moves each heart.
The very atmosphere is charged,
As quickly they depart.

In manger crude they find Him there,
God's Son now born of Mary,
Whose heart is filled with wonder still,
That she this Child did carry.

In thankfulness, they bend the knee,
Give thanks to God above,
For sending to unworthy man,
This greatest Gift of love!

IN SEARCH OF A STAR

There on that night so long ago,
The wise men sought for One,
Sent to earth by God, the Father,
His precious, only, Son.

God had sent a star to guide them,
To His humble place of birth.
O'er the stable did it hover,
There where Jesus came to earth.

There they found the lowly Savior,
As long ago foretold.
There they worshipped and adored Him,
Gave to Him their gifts of gold.

As the wise men came to Jesus,
So many years ago,
May it guide us to Him, also,
By following its glow.

May we hear God's message clear,
May this star still shine.
May we welcome Him to dwell,
In your heart and in mine.

WHY?

Why was He born in stable rude,
In lowly cattle stall,
To make His home with thankless man,
Come destined for the fall?

Why did He dwell with fishermen,
With tax collector, too?
And why endured the taunts of those,
Whose evil ways He knew?

Why did God, His only Son,
Send to this wicked earth,
To move among the worst of men,
And teach them of new birth?

Why did He walk a stranger here,
Despised, rejected, poor,
When heaven's riches all were His,
And angel hosts adored?

Why did He heal the leprous man,
And give sight to the blind?
Why did He feed five thousand there,
In pity for mankind?

Why did He in Gethsemane,
In deepest agony,
Pray, "Father, not my will, but Thine",
And sweat as blood for me?

Why did He hang upon that cross,
Forsaken and alone,
To there bear all of mankind's sin,
And for our debt atone?

Why did He come to give His life,
Such agony to know?
He came to die that we might live,
Because He loved us so!

PAULA, MY DAUGHTER

A daughter's something special,
None other can compare.
This treasure God has given me,
As gift so sweet, so rare.

I am so oft reminded
Of days when you were small.
You'd put your little hand in mine,
Your trust was all in all.

You're the little girl I cherished,
Precious child, to me so dear.
In my heart the mem'ries linger,
And again I wish you near.

Grandma loved "her girls" so much,
Her greatest treasure here.
She's waiting up in heaven now,
To draw them ever near.

Your sister's heart still longs for you,
She loves and misses you.
No on could ever take your place,
As you together grew.

I think of how in Sunday School,
"Your kids" you sought to teach,
To tell them of the Savior's love,
Their tender hearts to reach.

All too quickly you have grown,
Through swiftly passing days.
The hand that once gripped tightly mine,
Has reached in other ways.

The "Band Aids" that were often used,
Your little hurts to heal,
Are not sufficient, now, we know,
For all the hurts you feel.

We pray that you might know the joy
That serving God imparts.
To be what He would have you be,
Would deeply bless our hearts.

Never think that we don't love you,
How much you'll never know.
Although you may not see it now,
It will be ever so.

Each and every day I pray
God's love will reach to you,
And that His peace your heart will know,
And e'er to Him be true.

ARBUTUS (Beauty)

There's a flow'r that grows in the springtime,
It's fragrance fills the air,
It blooms in sweet exquisiteness,
Most delicate and rare.

A lady who's its namesake,
This flower puts to shame.
It counts it only honor
To have her bear its name.

Her time she's always there to share,
No matter what the task.
She's not too proud for any job,
No thanks she'll ever ask.

A special friend she's been to me,
She's always there to share
That deep concern upon my heart,
And help my burden bear.

She puts feet on her love for others,
Lip service isn't her style.
A helping hand she's there to give,
And go that extra mile.

So many sick and shut-in
Are in her tender care.
She shows a heart of compassion
And gentleness most rare.

To serve her God and fellow man,
To do what she can do,
A selfless life she ever lives,
A precious friend so true!

Her hands are those of a servant,
Her heart is one of love.
I pray that she'll, upon this day,
Be blessed by God above!

Written for 80th Birthday of
special friend, Beauty Pfeiffer.

A PRECIOUS FEW OF GOD'S 7,500 PROMISES

God's Book is filled with promises,
Oh, so great in number!
These promises I know He'll keep,
He'll never sleep nor slumber.

He's promised me a life that's more
Abundant, full and free,
And if the lilies so are clothed,
Much more He'll care for me.

If I will only cast my bread
Way out upon the deep,
He'll give a bountiful return,
And on me blessings heap.

He's said if I believe on Him,
He'll save me from my sin,
And if I His commandments keep,
He'll come and dwell within.

Old Satan's ever trying
To lure me far astray,
But God has told me to resist,
And he will flee away!

He's said if I pray fervently,
And seek with righteous heart,
My prayers will then avail me much,
And He'll His grace impart.

He's promised no temptation will
Be more than I can bear.
He'll ever be there to sustain,
He'll prove His loving care.

He's said He'll never leave me,
He never will forsake.
Nothing from His love can sever,
Or e'er His presence take.

A rainbow placed across the skies
Gives evidence He'll keep
His promise that He'll not destroy
The earth by waters deep.

Though weeping for this night endures,
He's promised morning joy,
A precious peace He gives to me,
Which nothing can destroy.

His angels He will send to care
For me, both day and night.
His watchful eye is ever there,
I'm always in His sight.

He's promised me a mansion fair,
Away beyond the sky,
And one day soon I'll take my flight,
To dwell with Him on high!

More precious grow these promises,
As through this life I go.
These things I can depend upon,
God's Word has told me so!

ETERNITY

This life once seemed to stretch before me,
Off' ring pleasures to my eye.
Dimmed my sight to things eternal,
And the thought that I must die.

My treasures here I fondly gathered,
Striving daily more to gain.
Still I found no satisfaction,
All my seeking was in vain.

God once again reminds me gently,
Life at best is quickly done.
All that we have here acquired,
Vanishes at setting sun.

There's a death that's everlasting,
Where God's presence never nears,
A great and mighty separation,
It's a valley filled with tears.

Satan ever seeks to lure us,
With the fleeting joys of sin,
Blinding us to life's hereafter,
Seeking wav'ring souls to win.

Eternity is never ending,
We must choose where we will dwell,
In the glory of God's presence,
Or the agony of hell!

God has loved us beyond measure,
And his precious Son He's giv'n,
Wounded hands are reaching toward us,
Yearning now to draw us in.

My Savior's precious blood was spilt,
There He died upon that tree.
He paid the ransom for my soul,
And from death did set me free.

I need to hold things lightly here,
For they soon will pass away,
To fix my heart on things above,
There in God's eternal day.

When ones I love are snatched away,
Gone my many dreams and plans,
My only recourse is in Him,
Placing all within His hands.

But He has promised better times,
In heaven's sweet tomorrow,
Where in His arms He'll hold me close,
And banish tears and sorrow.

Oh, wondrous day of revealed glory,
When my Savior I shall see,
Where with Him I'll dwell forever
In His blest eternity!

HAPPY FIRST MOTHERS' DAY
From Kristin Lee

Dear Mom, on this first Mothers' Day,
My heart is filled with love.
So, now I bring this love to you,
With thanks to God above.

He richly blessed me when He gave
Me such a special one,
Who's cared for me so tenderly,
E'er since my life's begun.

With words I cannot tell you now,
How much you mean to me,
But God in heaven knows my heart,
In its sincerity.

A special place there'll always be,
For you here deep inside,
And may it bring you joy to know,
'Twill last whate'er betide.

Now, even though I'm very small,
I'm sure that there's no other,
So worthy of the love I have
For my own dear sweet mother!

Written as if by Kristie for Lisa, her mother, on her first Mothers' Day.

GOD SENT A MIRACLE

Keisha Carol

In a tiny little bundle,
Came this precious child so fair,
Sent to me from God in heaven,
She's a miracle most rare!

Filled with wonder and amazement,
Now I touch the downy cheek,
Of this child entrusted to me,
Every feature so unique.

In sweet exquisiteness she lies,
So softly in my arms.
Dear Lord, Your guardian angel send,
Protect her from all harms.

Lovely eyes that now awaken,
Gazing deeply into mine,
Could be created by no other,
But a holy God divine.

He so perfectly did form her,
Made with love each tiny limb.
In gratitude, my heart's o'erflowing,
Now in praise and thanks to Him.

Lord, help me to be worthy of
This charge you've given me,
To give the guidance you desire,
To turn her heart to Thee.

Written following the birth of granddaughter,
Keisha, May 13, 1991, as if by her mother, Paula.

HE IS FAITHFUL

Why is it that I stand amazed
When once again He proves
He'll go beyond my fondest hopes?
In mighty ways He moves!

How can my heart so faithless be,
When o'er and o'er He's shown
His love for me in countless ways?
Such love I've never known.

How often He has answered prayers
I've even failed to pray.
He's drawn me back into His fold.
When I would go astray.

I've seen Him heal when hope was gone,
My heart in deep despair.
The Great Physician reassures,
We're ever in His care.

Sometimes the future's dark and bleak,
And trials press me sore.
What e'er may come to buffet me,
His grace He gives much more!

In situations where I fear,
Alone I cannot stand,
'Tis then He comes to shelter me
With His protecting hand.

JENNIFER - "BEANZ"

There's a little girl so precious,
A blessing giv'n to me,
By a loving God in heaven,
A spirit bright and free.

She's beautiful in face and heart,
Delightful to behold,
A precious life God's placed on earth,
More dear to me than gold.

She wears a smile to cheer my heart,
A face with joy aglow,
A thoughtful and a caring child,
Her love has blessed me so!

She's with her bright and sparkling eyes,
An angel in blue jeans,
The light and delight of my life,
She loves to be called "Beanz".

I pray for her a future bright,
That this sweet she will stay.
I pray God's blessing on her life,
With joys along her way.

Written for granddaughter, Jennifer.

MY MOTHER

Who on earth has loved me so,
To whom in trouble did I go,
Who else could such compassion show?
My mother.

A selfless, gentle lady, she,
Was always there to comfort me,
And shield me from adversity.
My mother.

She early taught me right from wrong,
Her hand so gentle, yet so strong,
With precepts to be held lifelong,
My mother.

A tender touch with loving hand,
A heart to always understand,
To be there meeting life's demand,
My mother.

And if she told me so, I knew,
The things she told me to be true,
And what she promised, she would do,
My mother.

She led me to belief in One,
Who's guided as life's race I've run,
And strengthened as each day's begun,
My mother.

She counseled me in times of strife,
To trust in God when fear was rife,
And take to Him these hurts of life,
My mother.

Upon her knees she brought me there,
Before His throne on wings of prayer,
Put in His hands my every care,
My mother.

I ever pray that I might be,
The mother that she was to me,
And that my children in me see
My mother.

MY PRAYER

I pray this season brings you joy,
And blessings rich abound.
May God be very near to you,
With love may He surround.

I pray that I may be a friend,
Some valleys help you through,
That your cares I might make my own,
And seek God's best for you.

May His strong arm give strength to you,
Each step along your way.
Any may my prayer be heard above,
For you and yours this day!

QUOTES

(In unorganized verse)

"It's amazing to me"
Is a phrase that we've heard,
To help him expound,
When he's teaching God's Word.

"The day and age in which we live"
Is called to our attention.
So many sinful things abound,
They're 'most too bad to mention.

"Since you asked the question"
He says now and then,
When making his point
On the answer depends.

He says he's a "Nice Guy",
We'd like to believe.
A preacher's not one
Who should seek to deceive.

"I won't take another offering,
This bit's a bonus free,
But if you'd like to treat to lunch,
T'would be all right with me".

These favored phrases that are used,
Serve "therefore" to endear.
So, Pastor Stephen, be aware
We're very glad you're here!

A tongue-in-cheek tribute to
Pastor Steve Beigle

REUNION

When I was young, they said to me,
The years would swiftly pass.
Their words fell then on doubting ears,
But now, alack, alas -

I know the truth of what they said,
Was it that long ago?
The date upon my calendar
Assures me that it's so.

When on occasion I may meet
A classmate that I knew,
It makes me stop and realize
That I've grown older, too.

Down through these years we all have gone
Our many separate ways.
We've had our trials and heartaches,
And also joy-filled days.

We're meeting now to reminisce
Of classmates - teachers, too.
To share what's happened in our lives,
And friendships to renew.

We're saddened by the loss of some,
With whom those years we shared,
That time of growth and learning,
For life to be prepared.

Janice Harvey

I thank my God for bringing me
Thus far along life's road,
For bringing us together now,
Time for a moment slowed.

Now may this class share memories,
Our hearts to closely bind.
May we be strengthened to go on,
And future years be kind.

SEASONED WITH LOVE

To each of you who took the time,
Your special dish to share,
We wish to dedicate this book
Of foods beyond compare.

With many favored recipes,
This volume's filled for you.
Some, so treasured through the years,
And some, so very new.

May every dish that you prepare
Be "Seasoned with His Love",
Received with praise and thankfulness,
From our dear Lord above.

We trust your palate will delight,
Your taste buds be inspired,
And each new recipe you try,
Leave naught to be desired.

As you prepare that tasteful treat,
That someone's shared with you,
Please pray that God might bless their life,
And with His love endue!

TREASURES IN HEAVEN

A precious gift called motherhood,
God places in our hands.
The care of these He's given us,
To mold them to His plans.

A treasure so immeasurable,
These to our hearts most dear,
A grave responsibility,
We have to teach them here.

Lord, may Your Spirit guide our hearts,
That we might guide to You,
Each precious child You've given us,
And keep them ever true.

I pray the words that I now speak,
The life that I here live,
Might plant a seed within a heart,
And heaven's harvest give.

What here on earth can give us hope?
Each thing will pass away.
Our great attainments are as naught,
Their joy but for a day.

The grave will lose its victory,
The sting of death be gone,
If all our treasures are above
In our eternal home.

A mother and a daughter there,
Are now awaiting me.
What precious hope God's promise gives,
That with them I shall be.

May each of us pass faith's baton,
In running now life's race,
That we may win that greatest prize,
And greet them face to face.

ODE TO UNCLE ARTIE

The time has flown so swiftly by,
The years so quickly passed,
These temporal things are so soon gone,
The love you've shown will last.

Our paths have far too seldom crossed,
Our lives too far apart,
Bu even with the miles between,
You've been within our heart.

The love you've shown to others here,
As on this earth you've trod,
Has touched their lived with blessedness,
And drawn them close to God.

If on this birthday we could share,
The warmth we feel inside,
We'd pray that through these future years,
God's peace with you abide.

TO BOB AND MILLIE

There are friends we've come to cherish,
Ones we hold so very dear,
Ones with whom we've shared the good times,
And we've sometimes shared a tear.

Friends like you are life's great treasures,
Precious gifts from God above.
Sent to give in some small measure,
Just a foretaste of His love.

Your faith in God has blessed your lives,
And those of us you touch.
You share your love in many ways,
Your caring means so much!

We're honored and we're privileged,
Your special day to share,
To join in celebration,
And lift you up in prayer.

The faith you've shared has been a bond,
That's helped the storms to weather,
It's strengthened you in times of stress,
And bound your hearts together.

On this, your anniversary,
We join with other friends.
To pray God's richest blessing,
And love that never ends!

GLORIOUS HOPE

May the One on this day risen,
Lift your heart to Him above.
May you know the joy and wonder
Of His blessed, saving love.

The cross on Calvary where they nailed Him,
But a token of their scorn.
Praise God, the cross and tomb are empty,
He arose that Easter morn!

May your heart receive Him gladly
He who suffered for your sin.
May you know the sweet forgiveness
Of the risen Lord within.

May your hope be ever strengthened,
Knowing that you, too, will rise.
The promise of His resurrection,
Eternal life with Him on high!

HE CONQUERED DEATH

Hallelujah! Christ is risen!
He who chose for me to die,
In humility He suffered,
Became sin for such as I.

Had I been earth's only sinner,
Bringing shame upon my Lord,
Still my pardon He'd have purchased,
That no other could afford.

Guilty, I, as those who shouted,
Crying loudly, "Crucify!"
As with them, the nails I pounded,
I, my Lord, did cause to die.

Even though I helped to slay Him,
Full forgiveness He has giv'n,
Filled my heart with joy unbounded,
Promised me a home in heav'n.

Suffering anguish there at Calvary,
All earth's sin and guilt He bore,
There, He felt Himself forsaken,
For me, He opened heaven's door.

Such great love, I cannot fathom,
Finite mind that I possess.
Though I too did scorn and mock Him,
Still He loves me none the less.

On the cross, all death He conquered,
There the victory was won.
Sin no more will have dominion,
We are ransomed by God's Son.

Filled with wonder and amazement,
Still I seek to comprehend,
Why He loved this worthless sinner,
Gave me life that knows no end!

RESURRECTION

The soldiers took Him from our midst,
Cruel hands upon Him laid,
They led Him to that judgment hall,
A mockery of Him made.

They put on Him a scarlet robe,
Placed in His hand a reed,
A crown of thorns upon His head,
And to His death agreed.

Pilate washed His hands of Him,
Said, "Do now as you will".
The cross was placed upon His back,
To bear up Calvary's hill.

The spikes they drove into His hands,
With spears they pierced His side.
His garments which they stripped from Him,
Amongst them did divide.

They hung Him there upon that tree,
His precious blood they shed.
Our fondest hopes asunder dashed,
For now our Lord was dead!

God's face was turned away from Him,
In this, earth's darkest hour.
The temple veil was rent in twain,
The earth shook by God's power.

In times when sorrow's overwhelmed,
His comfort sweet He's given.
A healing balm from His own heart,
And e'en a glimpse of heaven.

When friends have failed, and I have felt
Discouragement so deep,
In gentle arms He's cradled me,
And said, "My child, don't weep".

He's seen me through the meager times,
Sufficiently supplied,
My every need was fully met
When promises were tried.

Through all these many trials of life,
He's proven ever true.
May I commend this God of mine
To be a Friend to you?

With grieving hearts, we left Him there,
We could not bear such pain.
Life then so meaningless and bleak,
We'd ne'er see Him again.

They placed Him there in Joseph's tomb,
And sealed it with a stone.
They set a watch to make it sure,
Our fondest hopes were gone.

Our lives reduced to emptiness,
We went our separate ways.
We sought to find a meaning to
Those sad and grievous days.

How aimlessly we wandered then,
How could this really be?
He was to be our mighty king,
Now this cruel travesty.

When early on that morn we came,
The stone was rolled away.
The angels there proclaimed this truth,
"He is alive today".

Three days have passed since He was slain,
And torn from us apart.
Now Mary weeps beside the tomb,
And grieves with broken heart.

She turns to see a stranger there,
She thinks the gardener.
"Where have you laid my Lord," she asks,
Hope so faint within her.

His voice is filled with tenderness,
He speaks so softly, "Mary.
Go quickly now and tell my friends,
Make haste and do not tarry."

Unbounded joy now fills her heart,
Her risen Lord she sees.
In glorious triumph over death,
And falls upon her knees.

The day of victory has come,
Our Lord from death did rise,
And He will reign in majesty,
Away beyond the skies.

His resurrection is our hope,
Our hearts on things above.
We know one day we'll dwell with Him,
Enraptured by His love.

He lived, He died, He paid our debt,
None other could afford,
And now He lives forever more,
Our resurrected Lord!

TEACH ME TO PRAY

Lord, I ask that You would guide me,
As my heart seeks yours in prayer.
In an attitude of worship,
May I know Your presence there.

Now, help my heart to quiet be,
Through the tumult that abounds.
Grant me the peace that You can bring,
Though adversity surrounds.

May we share a precious moment,
Abba, Father, draw me near.
Take from me my doubting spirit,
Free me from the bonds of fear.

In intercession, Lord, I come,
Please do a work in me.
May Your Spirit bring me closer,
Let me be as one with Thee.

May I know Your loving presence,
Deep within my very soul
Tune my heart to be obedient
To Your guidance and control.

As quietly I bow before You,
Let me now Your will discern.
May I worship and adore you,
Teach me all You'd have me learn.

Help me, Lord, my praise to bring You,
Adoration from my heart.
Grant me deeper understanding,
May I see how great Thou art!

HE HURTS WITH YOU

God's promised He will ever be
Beside you whate'er trial you see,
And from its anguish set you free,
He hurts with you.

He'll be to you so very real,
When you to Him in faith appeal.
His arms around you, you will feel,
He hurts with you.

He knows the heartache that you bear,
His loving heart does ever care,
His Presence will be always there,
He hurts with you.

You'll never know a closer friend,
He's promised to His comfort send,
And walk beside you to the end.
He hurts with you.

His heart is touched with all your pain
Which now your very soul does drain,
But, trusting Him, new strength you'll gain,
He hurts with you.

May you now feel His arm of love,
Reach down to you from heav'n above,
And may His peace come like a dove,
He comforts you.

THE OLD TRUNK

Amid the dust and cobwebs there,
Upon that trunk I came,
And took a moment of my time,
My heritage to claim.

I looked upon that musty trunk,
And hoped that it could tell,
The secrets of its past to me,
Those things it knew so well.

As then I gazed upon that trunk,
I wished I could unfold
The mem'ries held so deep within,
And tales as yet untold.

There on the dusty floor it sat,
And no one seemed to care,
That it had known their hopes and dreams,
As they their lives did share.

How long ago, from Sweden's shores,
They chose to sail away,
To leave the homeland that they knew,
To seek a better way.

Belongings few were packed within
This trunk which now I see,
And loaded into steamship's hold,
To sail for country free.

A vision of a better life,
Within their hearts did burn.
With courage and with fortitude,
They sailed to ne'er return.

The voyage upon that steamer,
So many years ago,
Brought hardships to that stalwart pair,
Which few will ever know.

The trip was tiresome and long,
Confinement took its toll,
But still, they held their dream within,
And prayed to reach their goal.

They landed on this country's shores,
Their hopes now burning bright.
With joy and fear they looked upon
This new and awesome sight.

They settled here in Michigan,
Amid the Springvale hills,
Where from a spring, clear water flowed,
Through lovely rocks and rills.

To clear their land, to build their home,
To make their life together,
They strove with persevering strength,
And many storms did weather.

With diligence, he tilled the land,
His tools were far too few.
By hand, he made the harnesses,
With which the horses drew.

A skillful man upon his lathe,
Equipped with steady hand,
He whippletrees and eveners made,
So he could work his land.

A rolling pin still used today,
A product of his skill,
So oft serves to remind me how,
Each need he sought to fill.

He rose each day with dawn's first light,
And saw his tasks begun.
From sunrise until sunset red,
His day was never done.

A giant of a man he stood,
In stature, he was tall.
His shoes were made in size thirteen,
His strength was known to all.

He'd bear upon his shoulders strong,
A heavy laden barrel,
Held by his fingertips alone,
Up stairs both steep and narrow.

Two sons were born into this home,
And, also daughter fair,
Whom they endued with values strong,
And with them love did share.

His faithful wife, their children raised,
To teach them well she sought.
She kept her home with diligence,
Though with privations fraught.

With passing years, these children grew,
And left their childhood home,
To marry and begin anew,
With families of their own.

Their daughter dear, in childbirth lost,
To their hearts brought sorrow,
But still with courage, they pressed on,
To meet each new tomorrow.

The years so quickly passed away,
And age his strength had taken,
But he could say with honesty,
His goal he'd not forsaken.

With graying head and shaking hand,
His life now neared its end.
And then there came the day he took
His journey 'round the bend.

We, their children gather now,
To tighten family bond,
And also pay the homage due,
To those who've gone beyond.

So quickly families grow apart,
And go their separate ways.
All too often, ties are lost,
And closeness soon decays.

We come to reminisce today,
Acquaintance to renew,
To re-affirm our family ties,
And make new friendships, too.

My prayer is now that each of us,
Would seek to carry on,
And honor bring to family name,
With faith, our children don.

May we meet each future day,
Our trust in God kept strong.
May we uphold the values pure,
That did to them belong.

Alone, still sits their ancient trunk,
A name carved in its side.
And, we who gather here today,
Our tribute pay with pride!

A tribute to grandparents, Charles and Johanna Johnson, written for a family reunion.

THE LAMB OF GOD

This is He of whom Isaiah,
Prophesied in days of old.
This is He who came to save us,
One so long ago foretold.

He grew up like a tender shoot,
A root from out dry ground.
No majesty or beauty great,
In His form was found.

He walked this earth a stranger,
No place to lay His head.
He daily taught, He healed the sick,
The multitudes were fed.

The twelve He chose to serve with Him,
And for their strength He prayed,
But Judas, with deceitful kiss,
His precious Lord betrayed.

There alone in the garden,
He knelt in agony,
And lifting His heart toward heaven,
Prayed, "Take this cup from me.

'But, Father, not my will but Thine",
His all He yielded there.
For man's redemption willingly,
He chose our guilt to bear.

In Pilate's judgment hall He stood,
The mob cried, "Crucify".
Though he could find no fault in Him,
He sent Him forth to die.

To Calvary's hill they led Him then,
To treat with deepest scorn.
There on the tree they nailed Him.
His robe from Him was torn.

Incomprehensibly alone,
God's face was turned away.
The whole world's sin upon His head,
He bore it all that day.

His hands were pierced, the sword thrust in,
Upon that rugged cross,
A symbol of disgrace and shame,
For me He suffered loss.

God's precious Son He sacrificed,
His holy, sinless Lamb.
There He gave His best for me,
Unworthy as I am.

His grave was made there with the rich,
He with the wicked died.
Though He had done no violence,
He was unjustly tried.

Within the tomb they placed my Lord,
Secured it with a stone.
That grave, it could not hold Him there,
His Father took Him home.

The cross stands empty, He arose,
Sin's price was paid in full.
The aura of that cross was changed
From bleak to beautiful.

The worthy Lamb of God was He,
Who from the cross forgave,
The very ones who hung Him there,
And gave His life to save.

There He justified me freely,
On Him my sins were laid.
Oh, how my soul rejoices now
Because my debt is paid!

TO YOU WHO SERVE

With pride we think of you who serve,
To keep a country free,
Who put your lives upon the line,
To conquer tyranny.

In thankfulness we lift you up,
To our dear Lord above,
And ask that He'll protect and keep
You ever by His love.

My you reach out in faith to Him,
Who ever cares for you,
And trust that He'll be always near,
The conflict see you through.

We thank you for your willingness
To serve our country dear,
And for the courage you have shown,
With danger ever near.

May you have peace within your hearts,
And to your God be true,
Just lean upon His arms of love,
As they reach out to you.

His arm is never shortened,
His cause will never fail.
No matter what the strength of man,
God's will shall still prevail.

How deep the longing in your heart,
To feel a loved one's touch,
To see a tender smile upon
A face that means so much.

To hold a family close once more,
And know a home secure,
To peacefully lie down at night,
And of their love be sure.

As oft you're thinking thoughts of home,
Be sure we think of you,
And ever pray for your return,
That God will see you through.

We trust that day is very near,
When once again you'll be,
At home and safely dwelling in
This land of liberty!

THANK YOU

I thank the Lord for bringing you,
In a time of deepest need,
When our church was really hurting,
And we needed one to lead.

I'm sure God sent you to our church
To keep its heart alive,
To help us find our way again,
Through struggles to survive.

God's worked in mighty ways through you,
In reaching out in love.
His Word expressed in special ways
Brought insight from above.

You've not despised our humanness,
No "Holier than thou".
You've helped us understand God's will,
The why and when and how.

Your insight into what God's said,
My very soul has blessed,
And helped to calm my troubled heart,
And teach it how to rest.

The messages you bring to us
Are never, ever, dull.
No pretty, passive, platitudes,
Our consciences to lull.

Your vision for the future
Inspires us to press on.
It's rescued dreams we've had before,
When hope was almost gone.

Through struggles of our family
You've been a constant friend.
You were there in times of hurting,
When we couldn't see the end.

We frustrate you sometimes, we know,
Your patience we have tried.
The bafflement that you must feel,
You do so well to hide.

You've preached to us, you've picked on us,
You've made us laugh and cry.
We've been embarrassed many times,
And felt we'd like to die.

Through all these times of picking on,
We've still come back for more,
Somehow forgetting o'er again
We've been picked on before.

Linda's been a dearer friend
Than I ever could have known.
She's been someone I've leaned on,
God's love to me she's shown.

We love to have you in our home,
You're special, every one.
Love shows for all your family,
You're not too proud for fun!

I'm so glad Linda's heart is yours,
God brought you two together,
To love, encourage and sustain
Through storms you have to weather.

Each day I pray God's healing touch
Upon your throat, your voice.
To have them fully whole again,
Would make my heart rejoice.

And when you sing, God seems so close,
You've deeply touched my heart.
I pray He'll use this gift of yours
More blessings to impart.

Your friendship and your caring
Have meant so very much.
We feel as if you're "family",
You've brought God's special touch.

Your desire to live daily.
Ever, always, in His will,
Gives to us a constant challenge,
His commission to fulfill.

For Linda, Rob and Ryan, too,
I thank the Lord each day.
Sweet Amy's been a special gift
Of love along my way.

I pray that we might always be
Encouragers for you.
So many times you've strengthened us,
And helped us make it through.

We hope you'll stay "forever",
Our pastor, friend and guide.
You make God's Word so live for us,
He's ever at our side.

On this "Appreciation Day",
We want you all to know
How very much you mean to us,
We want our love to show!

"Pastor Appreciation Day" for
Pastor Steve Beigle

WITHIN THIS BOOK

Today I sought a quiet time,
Where pressures might release,
A time to sort my thoughts once more,
And gain an inner peace.

I picked a book from off the shelf,
And sat me down to read
The words penned by a wiser one,
To meet my deepest need.

And from a page within this book,
A heart reached out to mine,
With words of comfort I'd not known,
Filled full with love divine.

The wisdom to another given,
Which now they've shared with me,
Gives sweet new insight in my life,
My mind's unlocking key.

Lord, open now my seeking heart,
And help me to receive,
New truths that you've now shown to me,
And guide me to believe.

I thank you, Lord, that someone shared,
From deep within their soul,
A truth that you've revealed to them,
Which helped to make me whole.

WHAT HE'S DONE FOR ME

If I had a million years,
I still could only start,
To tell of all He's done for me,
This joy within my heart.

For me He's purchased with His blood,
A home in heav'n above,
Where I will share with all the saints,
The bliss of His great love.

He's been a friend when others failed,
When I'd nowhere to go.
He's lifted me from deep despair,
Because He loved me so.

He's gladly taken on Himself
My heavy load of sin.
He's washed the scarlet stain away,
And cleansed me deep within.

Through many trials still I have,
The peace He's given me.
He'll never leave me, nor forsake,
But always faithful be.

I can't begin to comprehend,
Why He for me would die,
But thankfully, I'll praise His name,
Until I'm home on high.

He's sometimes given heartaches,
Which I cannot understand,
But through it all He's promised
To hold me in His hand.

He's given friends and loved ones,
A fellowship most rare.
Supporting prayers have lifted me,
And shown how much they care.

He's given joy along life's road,
He's also given pain.
He asks me ever to endure,
That I might heaven gain.

He's given me some work to do,
And I must face my task,
To lead someone to faith in Him,
Before this life is past.

He's given me a burden for,
The souls of those I love,
That I might somehow point the way,
To faith in God above.

He's given me His Holy Word,
His promises so true,
To help sustain and guide me,
In everything I do.

He's given me a place where I,
May freely worship there,
And one who has a special gift,
His precious truths to share.

And now I patiently must wait
Until for me He'll come,
And take me home in heav'n to see
The final thing He's done!

AMY

I have a friend called Amy,
To me so sweet and dear.
My life's a little brighter,
Whenever she is near.

She is a special gift from God,
A ray of sunshine bright.
Her sweet and joyful presence,
Just makes the day go right.

One thing I hope to bear in mind,
Is "People more than things".
Just having lunch or playing games,
With her, such pleasure brings.

Every day I pray for her,
And I'm sure she prays for me.
I ask God's best in everything,
That in His will she'll be.

This verse has rambled long enough,
I'm sure you're bored by now,
But amateurish though it is,
I love you anyhow!

Written for Amy Beigle

CHOICES

Life is off' ring many pathways,
Both the good and bad are there.
Oh, how greatly it behooves us
Our pathway to choose with care.

We've not been promised ease of travel,
Difficult our way may be.
Joys and tears are sure to mingle,
As we're tossed upon life' sea.

But we have a blest assurance,
God will be there at our side.
If we're ever to Him faithful,
He will bear us through the tide.

May His loving hand uphold you,
Giving guidance as you go.
May you ever seek to please Him,
Just because He loves you so!

Written for graduation of Ryan Beigle

FRIENDS

If all my life would needs be spent,
Without someone to care,
If joys and sorrows came to me,
With no one there to share,

If some creation beautiful,
He brings within my view,
And my eyes only see this sight,
My eyes are yet too few.

If there were not a special one,
To take and hold my hand,
How could I bear my heartaches here,
With none to understand?

If there were no supporting hand,
To lift my heavy load,
And not a soul to wipe the tear,
I find along life's road,

How lonely then would be my path,
How empty my soul, too,
But God gives me a friend who will
My valley help me through.

I thank you, Lord, for knowing
That I need a human touch,
For sending me that special friend,
Whose caring means so much.

Thank you, Lord, for one who cares
Enough to pray for me,
Who helps direct my eyes toward You,
My comforter to see.

Then God in His great mercy comes,
And stays here by my side,
To strengthen and encourage me,
Though storms of life betide.

If I can squeeze the hand of one
Whose hope is wavering,
If I can give encouragement,
And to them comfort bring,

I pray that God might give to me,
An empathy so rare,
That I might give a heartfelt love,
And help their burden bear.

What special blessing He has giv'n,
When I with someone share
That little portion of my time
To let them know I care.

I thank you, Lord, for gift of friends,
As o'er life's road I've trod,
But, Oh!, what sweet reality,
My Greatest Friend is God!

ODE TO THE GREENS

We wish you joy upon this day,
These years together shared,
Have merged your hearts in unity,
Because you both have cared.

The years you've spent together,
The bad times and the good,
Will meld into God's plan for you,
As He has known they would.

Your children all are gifts from Him,
Each precious in His sight,
Enriching now your lives on earth,
As you embrace them tight.

Your futures, too, are in His hands,
As yielded to His will,
You chart your course together,
To prayerfully fulfill.

We wish you blessed future years,
Together on life's road,
With God's grace always with you here,
To lift your heavy load.

And now may love and joy and peace,
With both of you abide,
As you seek to do God's will
With Him at your side.

TO YOU WHO TEACH

To tell a little one of God,
To share His Precious love,
To have a part in building up,
His kingdom far above.

To give direction to a child,
Who may not know the way,
To point him toward the Savior,
That he may not go astray,

To take the time to love and care,
To build his faith in God,
Will in that day be worth it all,
When He gives His reward.

I'm priv'leged now to pray for you,
And for these ones you teach,
That God will truly use you,
As you seek their hearts to reach.

I thank Him for your willingness,
And pray that He will bless,
Your efforts now in His behalf,
As you His love profess.

May you see fruit of righteousness
In little lives and hearts,
As faithfully you seek to serve,
And He His truth imparts.

USE ME

Dear Lord, I pray that I might be
Someone who's used by You,
Who might declare to one who's lost,
Your promises so true.

Oh, make me ever conscious, Lord,
And train my eyes to see,
The hurting heart of one who needs,
A touch from You through me.

If there's a valley I've been through,
A stony path I've trod,
Oh, may I somehow share the strength,
That's drawn me close to God.

If I can only share a cup,
Of water clear and cold,
If I can give it in Your name,
And draw one to Your fold,

Then fill me with Your Spirit, Lord,
That I might with them share,
And tell them of the Savior's love,
And grace beyond compare.

Oh, give me deeper insight, Lord,
To truths within Your Word,
That I might help another learn
Of things they've never heard.

Where there is deep discouragement,
An aching heart somewhere,
Please make me willing, Lord, to give
The time to show I care.

If just a list'ning ear's required,
Help me to give that ear,
To hear what's on that heavy heart,
And help to banish fear.

A yielded life I owe to You,
And pray that it might show,
The joy that serving You can bring,
That others, too, might know.

To be what You would have me be,
To give what You require,
To be one truly used by You,
This is my heart's desire.

WAIT ON THE LORD

Please help me to be patient, Lord,
To see Your will be done,
For you to reach that one I love,
That their heart might be won.

There are those so dear to me,
For whom my heart would break.
I pray for them impatiently,
Lord, save them for Your sake.

Lord *now* is when I want to see
That loved one serving You,
To know beyond the slightest doubt,
That they'll to You be true.

Old Satan seeks to wear me down,
And says that God won't hear.
He tells me to no longer wait
For You to lend Your ear.

So often, Lord, I'd like to help,
And tell You what should be.
Why is it that I seem to think
You need advice from me?

Oh, Lord, it seems we wait so long,
To see a healing done,
To see relationships restored,
And walks with You begun.

To see Your church more perfect be,
Our vision now fulfilled,
To see Your great commission done,
And hope in hearts instilled.

To know the path You'd have me take,
Frustration in me grows.
Oh, give me clearer guidance, Lord,
Before this day should close.

How often I've wished vengeance wreaked,
Upon that hurtful one,
Whose bitter tongue and unkind acts,
Have caused such damage done.

You've told me, Lord, to wait on You,
Why can't I understand,
That in Your own much better time,
'Twill be done as You planned?

You've made it plain within Your Word,
That Your time is not mine,
But still I seek to hurry You,
Forgetting You're divine.

You've promised wings as eagles, Lord,
To those who wait on You,
That we shall run and never tire,
As You our strength renew.

Your purpose You will see fulfilled,
'Tis Yours but to command.
You know not haste, nor yet delay,
Each day is in Your hand.

Now, help me to be still and know,
You're ever on Your throne,
And that fulfillment there will be,
In *Your* time, not my own!

MARY

I remember a lady called Mary.
As one who loved her God.
Her greatest desire was to serve Him,
As on this earth she trod.

A humble life she sought to live,
No glory did she seek.
Instead to others honor gave,
With attitude so meek.

Her being o'er flowed with compassion,
Possessed with love most rare.
Whenever a soul was hurting,
A caring heart she'd share.

She'd always take the time to hear,
The troubles of a friend,
To share their load so heavy,
To help the heartache end.

She came to me to encourage,
When life was hard to bear.
She pointed my eyes toward heaven,
And One my load to share.

I did not know her very long,
Our paths had seldom crossed,
But when her Savior called her home,
A precious friend I lost.

You'd always see an inner joy
Reflected in her face,
Showing His redeeming love,
The evidence of grace.

When this life's trials were nearly done,
She knew the end was near,
But, still brought cheer to those around,
For herself, not a tear.

The peace she felt within her soul,
To other's hearts did give,
Encouragement to face life's storms,
And for their Lord to live.

She gladly took whate'er He sent,
Of sickness and of pain.
Her prayer was that her life might help
Another heaven gain.

She loved her family deeply,
Her greatest treasure here.
She's waiting now with open arms,
To hold them ever near.

Though from this earth dear Mary's gone,
We'll reminisce with love,
Until that glad reunion day,
When we shall meet above.

MY CHURCH

This is my church, most precious place,
Where God's love is so near.
A fellowship of kindred hearts,
A brotherhood so dear.

So oftentimes life baffles me,
With struggles that o'erwhelm,
Yet in His house, I feel a sense
Of comfort and of calm.

My broken heart, He seeks to heal,
If just to Him I'll yield.
He is the One all faithful still,
He is my Sword, my Shield.

His promises more precious grow,
As in life's storms I'm tossed.
There's empathy from caring hearts,
In times I've felt so lost.

This is where I hear God's Word,
Proclaimed with insight rare,
Where I can worship without fear,
And love with others share.

I think of those in other lands,
Whose faith such cost requires.
And humbly ask my God again,
To be what He desires.

With thankful heart, I praise Your name,
For Your upholding hand,
And for this place You've given me,
The freedom of this land.

I thank You, Lord, for loving me,
For wiping every tear.
Oh, may I ever worship You,
In adoration here!

HEAVEN

There's a place that my Savior's preparing,
A place called Heaven above,
Where I'll dwell with Him forever,
And share His deepest love.

Beyond the stars, I'll fly away,
And see Him face to face,
The One who gladly gave His life,
Who saved me by His grace.

So far away, and yet so near,
In a twinkling we'll arrive.
Our citizenship we'll gladly claim,
Up there beyond the skies.

I long for my inheritance,
The promised treasures there,
Where in my mansion I will dwell,
And walk the streets so fair.

Of sun and stars, there'll be no need,
God's Lamb will be our light.
In darkness we'll not wander there,
No more the shades of night.

Such rapture's in my heart instilled,
A joy that knows no bounds.
I long to hear the angels' song,
As it through heav'n resounds.

This glorious place is God's free gift,
In love for me prepared.
It's free because He paid the price,
Oh!, how much He cared!

How oft down here we wonder,
If anyone cares at all.
We feel unwanted and alone,
As on our knees we fall.

I won't be the last one chosen,
His love He'll share with all.
He'll take my insecurities,
And help me stand up tall.

There'll be no more thirst or hunger,
No suff'ring from the cold.
We'll know no want for anything,
When safe within the fold.

This place is for all God's children,
Though conflicts here we see.
It's big enough for all of us,
We'll dwell in unity.

Lord, help me to love my brother,
As much as You love me,
And realize he'll be there, too,
From diff'rences set free.

All facades will be forgotten,
No hidden heartaches there.
We'll know each other as we are,
Of pretence stripped so bare.

I'm just a'passing through down here,
And soon I'll take my flight,
To live with Him eternally,
My faith shall then be sight.

In the Bible, Paul has told us,
To leave this world is gain.
Our precious hope in heav'n above,
No more this life of pain.

Sometimes it seems our hearts will break,
In losing one who's dear,
But, God, His precious comfort sends,
And holds us ever near.

So many I've loved dearly,
Are waiting there for me.
What a time of sweet reunion,
When those dear ones I see.

The glory of Jesus' presence,
I long to comprehend,
To see His countenance so fair,
And know Him as my friend.

Each passing day, my longing grows,
To reach that heav'nly shore,
To live sublimely with my Lord,
In joy forever more!

IN MEMORIAM

In mind's eye now, we draw him near,
And hold him by our side,
These precious mem'ries that we share,
Will in our hearts abide.

A quiet man who loved his home,
A small house by a stream,
Where with his wife of many years,
He realized his dream.

So many simple things in life
Brought pleasure to his day,
From picking berries in the wild,
To fishing in the Bay.

The birds were friends he held so dear,
And daily fed them there.
His many dogs were "family", too,
With whom his life he'd share.

He chose to be a carpenter,
His trade he plied with skill.
Perfection always was his goal,
Commitment he'd fulfill.

To travel through this country great,
To camp beneath the pine,
To watch the twinkling stars at night,
Beneath them to recline.

From far Alaska's chilling snows,
To swelt'ring Texas plains,
He loved each climate that he knew,
From sun to drenching rains.

Alone in nature's peaceful realm,
Contentment he would find.
Believing God was in it all,
Brought comfort to his mind.

In quietness he lived his life,
In quietness he died.
A gentle soul, we'll miss him and
Remember him with pride!

- And A Few Poems

by Lisa

and

One by Paula

ARE YOU LIST'NING?

Are you list'ning, are you list'ning
To God's Word, what He says?
Strengthen one another,
Encourage your brother.
This I say, this I pray.

Lisa - 1990

LIFE BEGINS ANEW

God plants the seed that brings a flower,
Beginning life anew.
He shelters it with tender care,
Gives glory full and true.

God showers drops of morning dew,
And sets the brilliant sun.
He brings the moon to blackened sky,
When eventide is come.

God always seeks to calm the storm,
And guide us through the hour.
We see the glimm'ring light above,
Assuring of His power.

God give us hearts and lips to praise,
And hands to work and share,
To lift a voice up reverently,
With thanks to Him in prayer.

Written for Ladies' Spring Banquet - 1991
- Lisa

SPRING

Spring is like roses dancing on the lawn,
Spring is the birth of the new baby fawn,
Spring is a happy time of the year,
When all the new flowers soon will appear.

Spring is a time for the birds to return,
Spring is the time to clean and burn.
We are all happy and sunny and gay,
And all of the children - they jump, run and play.

Spring is a time for frolic and play,
When all of the bad times are cast away.
Spring is so beautiful and all of good cheer,
Let's hope it will be that way for all of the year.

Composed by Lisa, April 1978 - Age 11, for school.
Her teacher marked her paper "Excellent"
She submitted the poem to the "Big Boy Magazine"
and it was printed in their September, 1979 issue.

DEAR LORD...

I thank You, Lord, for giving me,
A gift called life, so full, so free.
A helping hand when I reach out,
In You I trust, I do not doubt.

I come to You in time of need,
T'is you my hungry soul will feed.
You're there for me, though night be long,
Your hand is gentle, yet so strong.

I cry, and You incline Your ear,
My deepest inner plea You hear.
When on tempestuous seas I sail,
You hold me strong against that gale.

I thank You now for Your great love,
And for my home in heav'n above.
I pray, dear Lord, that when I die
I'll rest with You at home on high.

Amen

Lisa

NANCY

God in His grace chose me to bless,
E'en though I deserved so much less,
So now to all I will profess,
You are my friend!

The reason why, I do not know,
He gave me you, His love did flow,
Most precious gift I treasure so,
You are my friend!

When life is stressed on every side,
Seems there's no place where I can hide,
But still I'm safe, I can abide,
You are my friend!

Oft times the road appears to bend,
When trials press, I see no end,
Then you to me your hand extend,
You are my friend!

If e'er I need a list'ning ear,
When eye o'erflows with silent tear,
You'll be there saying, "Do not fear",
You are my friend!

My thoughts and dreams with you I share,
Your needs I raise to God in prayer,
Remember, I am always there,
You are my friend.

Please know that with you I will stay,
Be close beside you all the way,
Should skies be dim, and clouds be gray,
You are my friend!

I can't see what God has in store,
But He will love us evermore,
We'll meet on His celestial shore,
You are my friend!

To special friend, Nancy Berends, March 1993
(Nursing Supervisor - Blodgett Hospital)

HAPPY BIRTHDAY, BEAUTY

Upon this very special day,
I just want you to know,
How very much you mean to me,
I'd like my love to show.

Your life o'erflows with empathy,
So very rich and rare.
You've been a special friend to me,
A gift that God did share.

If e'er I need a helping hand,
I know where I can go.
You'll ease the pain deep in my heart,
With love's bright radiant glow.

I've known you now, for many years,
When life seemed disarranged.
I'm glad to know that through it all,
You love has never changed.

You're a great friend to our family,
I've heard my sister say,
With admiration in her voice,
"Hope I'm like her someday!'

My mom and dad both love you so,
They only say the best,
Telling of all the good you've done,
With scarcely taking rest.

I feel it's such a privilege,
To be a friend to you.
Through you, the Lord has blessed my life,
His promises are true.

We've talked of heaven - all its bliss.
If one were to ask me,
I'd say the biggest star-filled crown
Would go to you, Beauty!

I LOVE YOU!

For Special Friend, Beauty Pfeiffer's 80th birthday,
September 1, 1992

JENNIFER

Her pretty, long, blond flowing hair,
And loving sparkly smile,
Mixed with innocent charisma,
Made everything worthwhile.

She from a little baby grew
Into a child so dear.
With strength she took on every day,
She knew that you'd be near.

I know that nothing can express
The sorrow which you feel.
I wish there were assuring words
That would your burden heal.

The questions always come to mind,
Of how, for what, and why,
Should God allow your precious girl,
So young an age, to die?

He had a sovereign plan for her,
That she a life would find,
In safe, secure heaven's realm
Leaving earth's pain behind.

We all will greatly miss her,
For you I now will pray,
That God's peace come into your heart,
And comfort you each day. – Lisa

Janice Harvey

"MEMORIES"

A shining smile in glistening eye,
The love that calms a fear,
The inner peace I treasure now
Whene'er I feel her near.

I knew when first I looked at her,
In lush green meadow's hue,
That I would be as she, someday,
With honor, love and truth.

A tall and stately rose was she,
Of morning dew adorned.
Her head held upward to the sky,
Approving, never scorned.

Then God allowed His miracle,
And thus began my life.
Petite, a bud on tiny stem,
I knew yet not of strife.

Small buds were nothing new to her,
She'd nurtured them before.
I was a touch of her grown flower,
She's held in days of yore.

She lived a full, rich, happy life,
Her children loved her dear.
'Twas she who taught me many things,
"Believe, and do not fear."

Soon my small bud full blossomed up,
And I became a flower.
I saw her head droop down a bit,
Her leaves reach out for power.

As daylight fades to moonlight shade,
Jesus came and touched her.
He took her home to heaven on high,
And with Him keeps her there.

A shining smile in glistening eye,
The love that calms a fear,
The inner peace I treasure now,
Whene'er I feel her near...

For Joey Nelson in tribute to her grandmother.
November, 1990 Lisa

MOTHERS

"What is a mother?", they'll ask me one day,
"A wonderful person," to them I will say.
"A mother is loving, helpful and kind,
She's the very best friend that you'll ever find.
Someone to look to, when you're feeling sad,
One who rejoices when you're feeling glad.
One whom you can trust and confide in, too.
She is always there, ready to help you.
A mother's sweet smile is something to cherish,
A glow on dark skies, which never will perish.
A mother's kind words can take away woe,
No other person ever loved you so.
So, when you are discouraged, despairing, distressed,
Remember your mother, because she is the best."

Lisa

MOTHER

I don't know where to start my praise,
Nor do I find an end,
To mother dear, a gift from God,
So wonderful a friend.

The time, it seems, has quickly flown,
As years go by and by,
No longer baby in your arms,
Sometimes it makes me cry.

Remember making gingersnaps,
With flour on my nose?
"The way a baker bakes," you said,
"That's just the way it goes."

The family's favorite summer spot,
Majestic Young State Park.
We walked the loops, and rode our bikes,
'Till it was nearly dark.

Marshmallows cooked o'er blazing fire,
And kielbasa, too.
Yes, memories fade, but never die,
Of special times with you.

I wanted only to be young,
"Thirteen", the perfect age.
Yet, followed I, in God's footsteps,
And let Him turn the page.

You've been there through the happy times,
You've seen me through the bad,
Shared strength and help and loving care,
When all of life seemed sad.

With me, you've shared Christ's boundless love,
His mercy and His care.
When there was no place left to turn,
To go to Him in prayer.

I say this all with heartfelt thanks,
For to me being true.
Please know that with my heart of hearts,
I always will love you ! ! !

Lisa

LET YOUR LIGHT SHINE

I saw a ship sailing
tempestuous seas.
He searched for a refuge,
a safe place to be.

The thunder kept rolling,
the rain showered down,
But still persevered he,
a harbor be found.

I watched as he wandered
with uncertainty,
In need of a lighthouse,
that tranquility.

I knew many of those
in places 'round here.
"Why have they no light on,
for one be in fear."

While I stood there pondering,
the Lord said to me,
"Where's your candle, my child?
Your brother's in need."

"Oh, it's here with me, Lord,
right here in my hand.
It helps me do Your work
good as any man.

'I'm in church each Sunday,
even Sunday School.
I pray for the missions
as a daily rule.

'I help those who need me,
see the Bible's read.
I wash the clothes for free,
I even make the beds!"

As I prided myself,
the Lord turned my eye,
To that ship in darkness,
with none to rely.

Realizing what I'd done,
I bowed down in shame,
Then I saw my lantern
had lost all its flame.

"Lord, I pray, forgive me
show me faith today,
To keep my light shining,
and lead those ships your way."

Written fall of 1990 - Lisa

UNTITLED POEM

Why did you take my father, God,
Why not just leave him here?
To him I'd go with troubled life,
With him I had no fear.

I know that You are sovereign, Lord,
I know that You are fair,
But let me prove my trust in You
With something else, somewhere.

When I was young, so small and frail,
I'd take my daddy's hand.
I'm sure he could do anything,
We'd conquer all the land.

The years have passed, You've let me grow
Into a woman now,
But, still, I'm weak as daddy's child,
I'm struggling - show me how.

My friends think so much time is gone,
For me 'tis but a day.
"It's been so long, I'm sure she's fine"
God, show them what they say.

Just maybe they're afraid to ask,
"Trish, don't you miss your dad?"
They might not want to speak for fear,
That it will make me sad.

I need to talk, to laugh and cry,
To share with you my heart,
Things precious, shared with dad, so dear,
That made it hard to part.

My husband has been wonderful,
He listens when I cry,
But, Lord, I still need other friends,
As earth's short days pass by.

I look toward that final day,
When daddy and I meet.
Please help me to be all you want,
Till this life is complete.

Found written on a notepad of Lisa's
for a friend named Trish.

LUGENE - GOD'S GIFT TO ME

God's grace o'erflows in boundless love,
His mercy knows no end.
He, through the years, has blessed me so,
With a most precious friend.

It wasn't just coincidence,
That day when first we met.
God, in His time, introduced us.
The time, the place, was set.

As time goes by, the more I see
Life's road unfolding still.
And marvel that His sovereign plan
Quenched needs, our hearts to fill.

You've been there when I've felt unsure,
When everything seemed wrong.
You've not condemned, have loved me still,
Assured me with a song.

I cry, you hear and you listen,
To me, incline your ear,
Remind me God is on His throne
"No longer need you fear."

Mere words alone can ne'er express
Just what you mean to me,
Of moments kept and treasures shared
Throughout eternity.

When this life's finished, all is done,
On heaven's shore we'll see,
Each other there with Jesus Christ,
Forever, friends we'll be.

HOPE

When the world is dry,
When the living things see no hope,
When the land is hot,
When the land thinks life is over,
Then comes the rain,
Soaking into the dry parched land,
Bringing new life and new hope
To all that's living.
So, when the world is dry,
The grass can hold on
And wait for the rain.

Paula Harvey
School Days

ABOUT THE AUTHOR

Janice Harvey resides in northern Michigan, with her husband, Jim, in the rural area of Charlevoix, on Susan Lake. Her writing has been a means of expression and release for her.

Two daughters were born to Janice and Jim - Lisa, who went home to be with her Lord on December 16, 1996, at the age of 29, leaving a daughter, Kristin, age 4. Their daughter, Paula Wager, lives in the same area with her husband, David, and their children Keisha, Brent and Jennifer.

Printed in the United States
1166500002B/361-411